KEEPING [barcode: T0275418]
A DIET FO

A Newly Revised Edition of
THE JEWISH
DIETARY LAWS

by
SAMUEL H. DRESNER

A revised guide based on
A Guide to Observance by
Seymour Siegel
David M. Pollock
Editor
Robert Abramson

THE RABBINICAL ASSEMBLY
THE UNITED SYNAGOGUE OF CONSERVATIVE
JUDAISM COMMISSION ON JEWISH EDUCATION

Copyright ©2000 by The United Synagogue of Conservative Judaism. All rights reserved. No part of this work may be reproduced without permission of the publisher, The United Synagogue of Conservative Judaism.

Keeping Kosher: A Diet For The Soul is a newly revised edition of *The Jewish Dietary Laws* by Samuel H. Dresner and *A Guide to Observance* by Seymour Siegel and David M. Pollock. Revised and Expanded Edition of *The Jewish Dietary Laws* copyright © 1982 by The Rabbinical Assembly of America and United Synagogue Commission on Jewish Education. Copyright © 1966, 1959, by the Burning Bush Press.

ISBN 978-0-8381-2105-4

ACKNOWLEDGMENTS

Rabbi Mayer E. Rabinowitz, Associate Professor of Talmud and Librarian, and Rabbi Joel Roth, Professor of Talmud, both of The Jewish Theological Seminary and sitting members of the Committee on Jewish Law and Standards of The Rabbinical Assembly, graciously gave of their time in reviewing the newly edited version of the "Guide to Observance" for this book. The Guide has greatly benefitted by their many suggestions on points of substance and style. The editor, in particular, wishes to express his appreciation for their assistance, while taking final responsibility for what is found in print.

FOREWORD

More than four decades ago, Rabbi Samuel Dresner wrote *The Jewish Dietary Laws*. Generations have probed the meaning of *kashrut* through this book and many have come to observe *kashrut* as a result of reading it. Rabbi Dresner wished to assure that it would continue to engage present generations so he revised it, rewriting sections and adding new illustrative materials. He even gave it a new title. All who have read a previous version and all who are presently exploring the meaning of Judaism for their lives will want to study this fresh look at *Keeping Kosher — A Diet for the Soul*.

Rabbi Dresner died as this book went to press. He had reviewed galleys and made corrections and additions even as his condition worsened. It was a great privilege working with him and learning from him. This work, as do his others, attests to his passion to make accessible to contemporary Jews the profundity of Judaism as a system of ideas, values and acts which makes claims on the way we live. In a very real sense, this book becomes a monument to his memory, זכר צדיק לברכה — the memory of the righteous is a blessing. Through his teachings, he has blessed us all.

Robert Abramson, Director
United Synagogue Department of Education
Editor

TABLE OF CONTENTS

THE PROBLEM OF UNDERSTANDING

Not Health But Holiness

Knowledge about *kashrut* (the Jewish dietary practice) is a mile wide and an inch deep. The dos and don'ts of keeping kosher so dominate any consideration of the subject, from rabbinical supervision to public consumption, that the deeper reasons are often unclear. Indeed, I would warrant that *kashrut* is more misunderstood than understood.

The most common misconception is that *kashrut* is an ancient health measure, which, while suitable in pre-modern societies, is an anachronism — given present-day methods of slaughtering, regular government inspection and sanitary food preparation — which should be discarded along with the horse and carriage and gaslight. But is health really the purpose of *kashrut?* Of course, *kashrut* includes concern for cleanliness and good health, but, again, is health its *primary* concern? Let us turn to the biblical text for an answer.

After we are told which animals, fowl and fish are permitted and which forbidden, the reason for this long series of laws is given in Leviticus 11:44-45:

> I, the Lord, am your God; sanctify yourselves therefore and be ye *holy*; for I am *holy*. . . . For I am the

Lord that brought you up out of the land of Egypt to be your God: ye shall be *holy* for I am *holy*.

Again, in Deuteronomy (14:21) we read:

Ye shall not eat anything that dies of itself ... ; for thou art a *holy* people unto the Lord thy God. Thou shalt not boil a kid in its mother's milk.

And finally in Exodus (22:30):

Ye shall be a *holy* people unto Me: ye must not eat flesh torn by beasts of the field: ye shall cast it to the dogs.

In each of these passages, dealing with three different aspects of *kashrut*, from three separate books of the Torah, the same word is repeated again and again: "holy" (in Hebrew: *kadosh*). Clearly, the purpose of the kosher laws is not health, but holiness.

To Be Holy Means To Hallow

What does holiness mean in Judaism?

Holiness stands in contrast to two other powerful words: *exploitation* and *escape*. These three terms — exploitation, escape and sanctification, or making holy — express three basic attitudes toward such central human drives as hunger, sex and the will to power. These three approaches are embodied, more or less, by three of the world's major spiritual forces: Paganism (exploitation), Buddhism/Early Christianity (escape), and Judaism (sanctification). Let us see how this is so:

> The way of exploitation worships the forces of nature.
>
> The way of escape denies them as sinful.
>
> The way of sanctification serves God by means of these forces.

Paganism glorifies our basic drives.
The Eastern religions and Early Christianity sub-
jugated them.
Judaism hallows them.

Exploitation says nature is holy and thereby un-
leashes the beast within us.
Escape says nature is unholy and thereby frus-
trates our natural desires.
Sanctification says nature is neither holy nor unholy, but *is waiting to be made holy* and it
thereby sublimates our natural desires to
the service of God through the *mitzvot*, the
commandments of the Torah.

Although formulated somewhat differently at different times and called by a variety of names, the pagan and
Eastern/Early Christian points of view have dominated
the thinking of humankind down through the centuries
to our own time. The revulsion to the shocking perver-
sions that marked pagan society's glorification of sex as
holy contributed to the later Early Christian degradation
of sex as sinful, which in turn produced and still produces
a renewal of the pagan view. As a pendulum swings from
side to side, so the way of exploitation and that of escape
have each provoked the sharp outburst of the other, one
extreme giving rise to the other.

Attitudes toward power may serve as a further example of the differences between these traditions. History knows both the worship of worldly power by the ty-
rant, as well as its rejection for the "alternative society"

of the monastery and the heavenly world by the Christian saint, or by the Buddhist holyman who trains himself to feel neither pleasure nor pain in his striving for Nirvana. The first case, where power is used to an evil end, is an example of exploitation; the second, where power itself is rejected, is an example of escape.

Judaism teaches a different way. In the words of Martin Buber, it:

> Teaches us to overcome the fundamental separation between the holy and the profane. This separation is basic to every religion. Everywhere the holy is set apart from the fullness of things and actions, so that the holy becomes a self-contained holiness outside of which the profane must pitch its tent. The consequence of this separation in the history of man is twofold. Religion is assured a firm province whose untouchableness is always guaranteed, but the holy is not given a corresponding power in the rest of life. In Judaism... one need only note the many everyday actions that are introduced by a blessing to recognize how deep the hallowing reaches into what is in itself unhallowed. One not only blesses God every morning on awakening because He has allowed one to awaken, but also when one begins to use a new house or piece of clothing or tool, because one has been preserved in life to this hour. Thus the simple fact of continued earthly existence is sanctified at each occasion that offers itself and therefore this occasion itself also.... The separation between the holy and the profane is only a provisional one.... In the Messianic world all will be holy.... The profane is regarded as the not-yet-hallowed. Human life is destined to be hallowed in

its natural form. "God dwells where man lets him in!" The hallowing of man means this "letting in." Basically the holy in our world is what is open to God, as the profane is what is closed off from Him, and hallowing is the event of opening out....[1]

The religion of Israel maintains that our world is neither to be deified nor vilified, neither glorified nor subjugated, neither worshiped nor despised. It is to be hallowed. And therein lies the challenge to humankind.

To Hallow the Everyday

In selecting as the central verse in the Bible, "Acknowledge God in all thy ways" (Prov. 3:6), the Talmud means to stress the word *all*. We can "acknowledge" God — that is, find God and serve God — not only in the synagogue or on the Sabbath, but in every act, every word, every place. All depends on *how* we act and *how* we speak. Thus, we may or may not serve God by the manner in which we talk to our spouse, cast our ballot, fill out our income tax return or treat our employee or customer. In each case we may minister to the Lord by hallowing our action, that is, by performing each deed in such a way as to advance the kingdom of Heaven on earth. When there is love and devotion between husband and wife, marriage is hallowed; when we vote for the ability and integrity of a candidate and not the favors we may win, we hallow our country; when we deal fairly with our employee, we hallow our business. It is the duty of the Jew to raise up all of life to God, *to hallow the everyday*.

To the question, "How does a human being strive to become holy?," other religions might answer: by having the right feeling or belief or by self-denying acts. The common association of self-denial with holiness is illustrated by an event Rabbi Abraham Heschel once related to me. In conversation with a Hindu philosopher, the latter observed: "I have heard of your Sabbath; it is so holy a day, surely you must fast on it!"[2]

Judaism would agree that feelings and beliefs are central to holiness, but it would likewise assert that the struggle for holiness does not begin there. Judaism concerns itself with more than the Sabbath or the synagogue or ritual or right belief. On the contrary, its great claim, as expressed from the Bible to the latest responsum is that faith — encompassing the entirety of one's life, affecting all of our days or none of them; being relevant to our total manner of living or to none of it — is just as concerned with the seeming trivialities as with the exalted aspects of one's existence.

Indeed, Judaism would argue that it is precisely with these seeming trivialities, the habitual and apparently inconsequential, that we must commence in order to create the holy person. And what is more common, more ordinary, more seemingly inconsequential than the process of eating? It is precisely here that Judaism would have us begin the task of hallowing the everyday. For how we approach food may be more significant than reflecting on a dogma. It may be more important to say *Hamotzi* (the blessing for eating bread) with *kavanah* (devotion) than to memorize a creed. Make something fine and decent out of the common practice of eating and you will have taken a step toward holiness. More important than what one thinks, Judaism teaches, is what one *does*. Proper thinking may, in fact, follow proper doing, attitudes deriving from activities. Responding to the question: why, in accepting the covenant with God at Sinai, the people-Israel said "*na'aseh v'nishma*," "we shall do and we shall hearken," instead of the reverse —should not "hearkening" precede "doing"? —the Ba'al Shem explained that "in the doing is the hearkening."

Now, we can better understand the *mitzvah,* the commandment, of *kashrut.* We are commanded in Scripture to be a holy people: "Thou shalt be holy for I the Lord thy God am holy" (Lev. 19:2); "Thou shalt be a kingdom of priests and a holy nation" (Ex. 19:6). Again and again the people-Israel is commanded to be holy. But how is holiness achieved? For it is not a genetic inheritance like the color of our eyes or the length of our frame. We become holy through our own effort and with God's help, by hallowing that which is not yet holy, the profane, the everyday. And that is the labor of a lifetime. It is realized, Judaism teaches, through the observance of the *mitzvot.* The first words of the blessing we say before doing a *mitzvah* remind us: "Blessed art Thou 0 Lord our God, Sovereign of the world *who hallows us when we perform Thy mitzvot....*" *(Barukh Atah Adonai Elohenu Melekh ha-olam asher kid'shanu b'mitzvotav...).* The *mitzvah* of *kashrut* helps us hallow the act of eating. By making holy, the people-Israel takes on an aspect of holiness.

Ennobling our way of eating, however, is no simple achievement. After all, eating is a function we have in common with the animals, and, in this respect, there are those who are not greatly different from animals approaching their meal with the same single-mindedness and gluttony. To sit at their table is to endure a litany of comments about food served at this or that club, this or that restaurant, this or that party; of the need for dieting and the helpless habit of overeating. Still, matters have not reached the pagan, Roman practice of placing a bowl at the end of each row of the amphitheater, appropriately called a *vomitorium*, into which one could empty one's stomach, in order to refill it yet again! Our modern displays may be more sophisticated but are not really different in essence. The pagan glorification of elemental needs is still very much with us.

Conversely, the Buddhist/Early Christian attitude was one of ascetic denial of bodily desire. The soul, not the body matters; not this world, but the world to come. True, food is a necessity for life, but one must take care not to enjoy it overmuch. Humans, they taught, are sinful creatures who cannot curb their lust, beasts unable to obey God's law. Therefore, asceticism often characterizes these religions.[3]

Judaism, too, has a place for fasting among its tenets, but it is a limited place. While Jews are commanded to fast on Yom Kippur, they are likewise commanded to eat on the day before Yom Kippur. As if to emphasize this, the Sages wrote, "If one eats and drinks on the ninth day of the Hebrew month of *Tishri* (the day before Yom Kippur), it is as if he would fast on both the ninth and tenth days of *Tishri.*" To this a later Rabbi remarked: "Thus we are taught that while it is difficult to fast for the sake of heaven, it is even more difficult to eat for the sake of heaven."

Judaism rejects both the pagan exploitation of the elemental need for food, as well as the asceticism of Early Christianity/Buddhism. History has swung as a pendulum from one extreme to the other. Readers may judge for themselves at which point in the pendulum's stroke we find ourselves today.

Judaism teaches a third way. It says that God created the world and made humans in God's image, that we are given the power to discover God's will and to obey it, and that our task is neither to escape from the world nor to worship it. With the Torah as a vision and the *mitzvot* as a path, we can strive to fulfill God's dream for creation. It says that we have the power to hallow the act of eating, that we can find a way of ennobling and raising this prosaic routine which will lend it an aspect of holiness, a means of serving God. For we are not merely animals, or even, as Aristotle would have it, animals with a mind. Humans are better defined as *religious* animals blessed with the power to transform their brute functions. The glory of humans is their power to hallow. Even the act of eating can be hallowed; even the act of eating can become a means for achieving holiness.

Kashrut, therefore, may be defined as Judaism's attempt to hallow the act of eating by teaching us reverence for life.

Eating Meat: A Divine Compromise

How does *kashrut* hallow the act of eating?

Kashrut teaches, first of all, that the eating of meat

is a *compromise*. To many it will come as a surprise that
Adam and Eve, the first humans, were not permitted to
eat meat. Yet we have only to look closely at the biblical
text to see that this was surely the case.

> And God created man in His own image, in the im-
> age of God created He him; male and female cre-
> ated He them. And God blessed them; and God said
> unto them: "Be fruitful and multiply, and replenish
> the earth and subdue it; and have dominion over
> the fish of the sea, and over the fowl of the air, and
> over every living thing that creepeth upon the
> earth." And God said: "Behold, I have given you ev-
> ery herb yielding seed, which is upon the face of all
> the earth, and every tree, in which is the fruit of a
> tree yielding seed — to you it shall be for food! (Gen.
> 1:27-29).

So we see that the diet of Adam, the first man, who
dwelt in the ideal society of the Garden of Eden, is limited
to fruits and vegetables. He is meant to be a vegetarian.
No mention is made of animal-food, only "every herb yielding seed" and "every tree in which is the fruit of a tree
yielding seed." Not until we come to the story of Noah is
meat permitted:

> And God blessed Noah and his sons, and said unto
> them: "Be fruitful and multiply, and replenish the
> earth. And the fear of you and the dread of you shall
> be upon every beast of the earth, and upon every
> fowl of the air, and upon all wherewith the ground
> teemeth, and upon all the fishes of the sea: into
> your hand are they delivered. Every moving thing
> that liveth shall be for you; as the green herb have I
> given you all. Only flesh with the life thereof, which
> is the blood thereof, shall ye not eat (Gen. 9:1-14).

Adam and Eve are forbidden meat; Noah is permitted it. Why? What intervened between the generations to bring about such a change? The answer, of course, is sin. Adam and Noah both represent man: Adam in his ideal state in the Garden of Eden; Noah in his real state outside the Garden of Eden. Adam proved unfit for paradisal society. He had rebelled against God and was driven from the Garden. Did his rebellion include the rejection of his limited vegetarian diet in favor of the more tasty meat choices? And was he prepared to go to the length of taking the life of the animal? It would seem so. For Noah was no longer guided by the dietary restraints of Eden, and it remained so for his descendants. Ideally, humans should not eat meat, for to eat meat, the blood of a living creature must be shed. But humans will eat meat. It is their desire and, perhaps, too, their need.

Just as at the beginning of time there was no eating of meat in the ideal society of the Garden of Eden, so at the end of time there will be a return to the original state in the perfect society described by the prophet Isaiah:

> And the wolf shall dwell with the lamb,
> And the leopard shall lie down with the kid,
> And the calf and the young lion and the fatling
> together,
> And a little child shall lead them.
> And the cow and the bear shall feed,
> Their young ones shall lie down together,
> And the lion shall eat straw like the ox.
> They shall not hurt nor destroy in all My holy mountain;
> For all the earth shall be full of
> The knowledge of the Lord,
> As the waters cover the sea (Isaiah 11:6,7,9).

Included in the prophet's description of the future perfect society, where all conflict within nature will give way
to peace and harmony, is the striking statement that the
lion (along with the wolf and the leopard) shall no longer
live on the flesh of other beasts but, like the domesti-
cated ox, eat the growth of the field. And can we, therefore, not draw the inference that if the fierce, carnivorous beast will be so transformed in the future messi-
anic society, how much more so the carnivorous human?
If bloodthirsty animals will themselves no longer devour
other animals but live on fruits and vegetables, even
straw, how much more so man? It seems quite evident
that the prophet believed that, in the future time, humans, too, will no longer eat meat. "The biblical account
of the scheme of human destiny represents it as a tem-
poral process with creation and the paradisal state at the
beginning and redemption in the Kingdom of God at the
end. In between is history" (Will Herberg). At the "beginning" and at the "end" humans in their ideal state are
herbivorous. Human life is not maintained at the expense
of the life of the beast. In "history," however, which takes
place here and now, and in which humans with all their
frailties and foibles live and work out their destiny, we
may be carnivorous.

Human consumption of meat, requiring the taking of
an animal life, has constantly posed a religious problem
to Judaism. The Rabbis of the Talmud were aware of the
distinction in the matter of food between man's ideal and
his real condition. Referring to Deuteronomy 12:20, they
said:

The Torah teaches a lesson in moral conduct,

namely, that man shall not eat meat unless there
is a special craving for it, and shall eat it only occa-
sionally and sparingly.... Only one who studies Torah may eat meat, but one who does not study Torah is forbidden to eat meat.... Once Rabbi Judah
the Prince taught Torah before an assembly of Jews
at Sephoris in Babylonia, and a calf being led to the
slaughter passed before him. It sought to hide itself
in his cloak and began to cry, as if to say: "Save
me!" "What can I do," thought Rabbi Judah, "since it
is for this that you were created?" It was therefore
decreed in heaven that because he had no compassion, sufferings should come upon him. One day a
weasel ran past his daughter and she wanted to kill
it. He said to her, "Let it be, for it is written, 'His
mercies are over all His works (Ps. 145:9).' So it was
decreed in heaven that because he had pity, pity
should be shown to him. And his sufferings ceased.[4]

A striking incident is recorded in the biblical book of
Numbers. Although the people were carrying the tablets
of the ten commandments received at Mount Sinai and
were on their way to the promised land, their long trek
through the barren wilderness tried their patience and
led to a series of revolts. One of the most serious of these
revolved around the lack of meat. Listen to the Torah's
graphic description of the event.

The riffraff in their midst felt a gluttonous craving; and then the Israelites wept and said, "If only
we had meat to eat!.... Our gullets are shriveled,
for there is nothing but this manna to look to!"...
The Lord was very angry, and Moses was dis-
tressed.... Moses said to the Lord... "Where am I to
get meat to give to all this people, when they whine

before me and say, 'Give us meat to eat!'.... It is
too much for me... Kill me, and let me see no more
of this wretchedness!"
Then the Lord said to Moses.... Say to the people:
..."Tomorrow ye shall eat meat, for ye have been
whining, 'If only we had meat to eat! We were better off in Egypt!' The Lord will give you meat and
ye shall eat meat... until it comes out of your nos-
trils and becomes loathsome to you. For ye have
rejected the Lord... by whining, 'Oh, why did we
ever leave Egypt!".... [And] while the meat was
still in their mouth, the anger of the Lord blazed
against them and a severe plague struck them.
That place was called *Kibrot-hata'avah*, the graves
of craving (Numbers 11:4-15;18;33-34).

In dealing with the question of eating meat, the Rabbis distinguish between *b'sar kodshin*, holy meat — part
of which first had to be offered as a sacrifice in the Tabernacle by the Israelites and only then was it permitted to
be eaten — and *b'sar ḥulin*, profane meat — meat which
was eaten even though it had not first been brought to
the Tabernacle. *B'sar ḥulin* was permitted to the people
only after they had left the wilderness and entered the
land of Israel, when the population multiplied, a central
Sanctuary was established and it became difficult to travel
to the Sanctuary. It is, however, the term they gave to
this profane meat which is striking. They called it *b'sar
ta'avah*, the meat of lust or luxury, after the passage in
Deuteronomy 12:20:

When the Lord thy God shall enlarge thy border,
as He hath promised thee, and thou shalt say: "I
will eat flesh," because thy soul lusteth to eat flesh;

thou mayest eat flesh, after the lusting of thy soul.
If the place which the Lord thy God shall put His
name there [i.e., the Sanctuary] shall be too far
from thee, then thou shalt kill of thy herd and of
thy flock, which the Lord hath given thee, as I have
commanded thee, and thou shalt eat within thy
gates, after all the lusting of thy soul. .... Only be
steadfast in not eating the blood; for the blood is
the life; and thou shalt not eat the life with the
flesh. Thou shalt not eat it. Thou shalt pour it
out upon the earth as water. Thou shalt not eat it;
that it may go well with thee, and with thy children after thee, when thou shalt do that which
is right in the eyes of the Lord (Deut. 12:20-21,
23-24).

The permission to eat meat is thus understood as a
*compromise, a divine concession to human weakness and
human need.* The Torah, as it were, says: I would prefer
that you abstain from eating meat altogether, that you
subsist on that which springs forth from the earth, for to
eat meat the life of an animal must be taken, and that is
a fearful act. But since you are not perfect humans, and
your world is neither a Garden of Eden nor the Kingdom
of Heaven; since your desires cannot be halted nor your
nutritional requirements altered, they must at least be
controlled; since you will eat meat and since, perhaps,
you need to eat meat, you may eat it, but with one re-
striction — that you have reverence for the life that you
take. "The flesh with the soul thereof, which is the blood
thereof, shall ye not eat" (Gen. 9:4).

Reverence for the Life We Take

Jews are permitted to eat meat, but they must learn to have reverence for the life they take. Reverence for life is an awareness of what we are about when we engage in the simple act of eating flesh. It is a constant lesson of the laws of *kashrut.*

The manner of slaughter, *sheḥitah.* The laws of *sheḥitah* found in the Talmud go back, at least in part, to the Bible, as the following verse seems to imply, "Thou shalt kill of thy herd and thy flock which the Lord hath given thee, *as I have commanded thee*" (Deut. 12:21). The words, *as I have commanded thee*, suggest that a special manner of slaughter existed in biblical times.

The laws of *sheḥitah* provide a humane method of slaughtering animals. Great care is exercised that the knife be regularly examined before and after it is used to determine that it is especially sharp and perfectly smooth, without a notch that might tear the flesh. The cut severs the arteries to the head of the animal, thereby stopping circulation to the brain and rendering the animal unconscious of pain. This is not true when the animal is only stunned by a blow.

Further, the one who slaughters the animal, the *shoḥet,* must be carefully chosen. He not only must slaughter the animal according to Jewish law but is obliged to examine its internal organs to make certain the animal is not diseased. Among non-Jews, work in slaughterhouses is usually performed by a lower level of society, uneducated, rough men. With Jews it is otherwise. The *shoḥet* must be both learned and pious. He must pass an examination attesting to his thorough knowledge of the religious laws relating to his work and is obliged to recite a blessing before he executes his duties, ever reminding him of the seriousness of his labor, behind which is the somber teaching of *kashrut* as a divine concession. All this works against brutalization. "Thou shalt kill of thy herd and thy flock which the Lord hath given thee, as I have commanded thee" (Deut. 12:21), that is, we may slaughter an animal for food, but only *as I have commanded thee*.[5]

Kashering, the removal of blood. A central purpose of the laws of kashering is the removal of the blood. It is not enough that the animal must be killed in the most humane way, but the symbol of life, the blood, must be drained, for blood is the symbol of life. Man is forbidden to shed blood: "Whoever sheds the blood of man, for that man shall his blood be shed. For in the image of God was man created" (Genesis 9:3-6). Noah and his sons are told that while the animal may be eaten, the blood may not: "Only be steadfast in not eating the blood; for the blood is the life; thou shalt not eat the blood with the flesh" (Deut. 12:23-25; also Lev. 17:11; cf. I Sam. 14:32-34). Jacob Milgrom, a contemporary biblical scholar, summarizes: "Man must abstain from blood: human blood must not be shed, and animal blood must not be ingested."[6] In addition, removal of blood serves as a sacrifice by denying the palate the more tender, tasty flesh, and serves to remind us once again that the whole act of eating meat is a concession and a compromise — a further exercise in reverence for life.

Limitation of animals to be eaten. Because we are permitted to eat meat only as a compromise, a divine concession to human weakness and need, animals which are *n'velah* (that which dies of itself) or *trefah* (that which is killed by another animal) are forbidden. Such animals have not been killed according to Jewish law, which procedure attempts to show reverence for the life it takes and renders them permissible for food. Only animals so treated may be eaten. Animals found to be diseased upon examination by the *shoḥet* are declared *trefah*. Furthermore, only tame, domestic animals which are herbivorous can be eaten. Also, the especially fierce species of carnivorous fowl, such as the hawk and eagle, are forbidden.

The Larger Meaning of Reverence for Life

The reverence for life which *kashrut* teaches has a larger meaning. It is a meaning yet to be appreciated by a society as bloodthirsty as ours.

Hunting. In a discussion on the morality of hunting, the critic Joseph Wood Krutch commented that ordinary killers "are selfish and unscrupulous, but their deeds are not gratuitously evil. The killer for sport has no such comprehensible motive. He prefers death to life, darkness to light. He gets nothing except the satisfaction of saying, 'something which wanted to live is dead. There is that much less vitality, consciousness, and, perhaps, joy in the universe. I am the Spirit that Denies.' When a man wantonly destroys one of the works of man we call him Vandal. When he wantonly destroys one of the works of God we call him Sportsman." The zoologist H. E. Anthony, who defended hunting in the same discussion, admits "that a basic inconsistency underlies the shooting of game. No one will deny that there is an inconsistency in cherishing a beautiful dog for many years and going out every fall to shoot an equally beautiful deer. But, so far as we know, there is no escape from the tension of inconsistencies of which life consists."

The reason why the world has never adopted the opinion of a Krutch is because there has always been an Anthony who throws up his hands in despair over the apparently uncontrollable killer instinct in man. But is not controlling brutal impulses what civilization is all about? If it is discouraging to consider the popularity of such pastimes as cockfighting and bullfighting, banned in the United States, to which eager spectators gather to thrill over a bird torn to pieces or an animal pierced with a blade, what shall we say of American prizefighting, where the crowd, bored at the most skilled exhibition of boxing, waits only for the "killing." Spectators may recoil for the moment at the grisly attempt of one fighter to chew off the ear of another, but trample down the gate to see a rematch; and what hockey player's face is not marred with stitches and broken teeth, the evidence of aggressive plays and fighting cheered on by the crowd?

The Jew is taught to view such cruelty, especially the deliberate shooting of an animal for no reason other than "sport," with utter abhorrence. He knows that in the repeated act of killing animals, a gradual demystifying of life occurs. Responding to this danger, Judaism offers

neither pious platitudes of condemnation nor sterile expressions of helplessness. The laws of *kashrut* serve as a
system of spiritual discipline which attempts to train the
Jew each and every day in reverence for life, by restrict-
ing the kinds of animals which may be eaten, providing a
humane manner of slaughter and a trained slaughterer.
It is of interest to note that the hunter and the knight,
heroes of gentile society, were often depicted in Passover
haggadot as the "wicked son."

The lessons of reverence for life became so ingrained
in the people-Israel, due in good measure to the practice
of *kashrut*, that even those distant from religious observance retained an aversion to cruelty to living creatures.
Albert Einstein, when asked to define the spirit of the
Jewish tradition, responded by citing a remark of his
friend, Walther Rathenau, the noted German patriot and
assimilated Jew (assassinated in 1922 when foreign minister of the Weimar Republic): "If a Jew says he enjoys
hunting, know that he is lying!"[7]

Birds. Concern for the feelings of God's creatures finds
rich expression in Judaism. Take the case of birds, for
example. Scripture warns that should one come upon a
bird's nest with the mother-bird and her fledglings or eggs,
one may not take the mother along with her young, but
must first let the mother go, and then take only the young,
"that you may fare well and have a long life" (Deut. 22:6).
In the Noah story it is the bird which first rests on dry
land. This bird, thought to be a dove because it is mo-
nogamous (as Israel's love of the Lord should be), is lik-
ened to Israel who likewise is small, fragile, soars heav-

enward, and, as the Sabbath table-song has it, finds the respite of the Sabbath day as the dry land amidst the flood waters of history.

When the Israelites crossed the Red Sea, the birds accompanied them with song, and in remembrance, each year a Sabbath of Song is celebrated, marked by the children leaving breadcrumbs for the birds. The story is told of the arrival in 1941 of a Polish Jew into the port of Haifa carrying a birdcage. Asked why, under such harrowing conditions, he could bother with baggage so cumbersome as a birdcage, he replied that the Jewish children of Poland were being slaughtered and there would soon be no one to look after their birds.

How reverence for life reflected itself in the character of the Jewish people is the subject of a story about birds by Sholom Aleichem, the master-artist who best pictured Jewish life in Eastern Europe. It is the tale of two children, one Jewish and the other gentile, whose friendship begins to break down over the issue of sensitivity to helpless creatures, common to Jews but not so common to the non-Jews of the time. The difference was the tradition of the Jewish people, which taught reverence for every living creature. The two friends had not seen each other over the severe winter and met for the first time shortly before Passover. They were full of news for one another. Feitel, the Jewish boy, boasted that during the winter he had learned the Hebrew alphabet from beginning to end. The gentile, Fedka, on the other hand, boasted that he had been given a whip. Feitel reported how his father took him to town where he saw the great synagogue. Fedka told how he tried to get at a bird's nest, and could not; so he threw stones until he had killed the baby birds.

"Did you kill them?" cried Feitel, horrified.

"They were little ones," Fedka explained.

"But you killed them?"

"They didn't even have feathers; only yellow beaks and fat bellies."

"But you *killed* them?

The evil of killing defenseless creatures cannot be mitigated.

Animals and fish. The many laws in the Bible and Talmud teaching kindness to animals find formulation in the single rabbinic dictum, *"tza'ar ba'alei hayim,* [be on guard against] cruelty to any living creature," a phrase absorbed into the Yiddish folk idiom of the people. The evidence of such an attitude is considerable and ancient. Consider the following teachings: ploughing with a bull and a donkey harnessed together is forbidden, because they are not equal in strength and the weaker would suffer in trying to keep up with the stronger (Deut. 22:10); while treading out the corn, the ox (or any other animal) cannot be muzzled (Deut. 25:4); when an animal is born, it is not to be taken away from its mother for at least seven days; an animal and its young must not be killed on the same day, lest through thoughtlessness the young is killed in the presence of the mother. "For ye shall keep My commandments, and do them... And ye shall not profane My holy name; but I will be hallowed among the children of Israel: I am the Lord who hallow you... I am the Lord" (Lev. 22:26-33). Before one is permitted to sit down at table to eat a meal, the Talmud says, one's animals must first have been fed. Finally, the great law of the Sabbath forbidding work one day in seven was revolutionary in the eyes of the ancients, especially so, since the law embraced not only the Hebrews but their servants, their slaves and even their animals. "The seventh day is a Sabbath unto the Lord thy God; in it thou shalt not do any manner of work — thou, thy son or daughter, thy male or female slave, nor thy stranger within thy settlements, *nor thy cattle*" (Ex. 20:8-10). A popular legend of the talmudic Rabbis recounts how a pagan was angered every seventh day when his healthy, newly purchased animal refused to work. He had bought it from a Jew!

Reflecting the sentiments of these laws regarding the welfare of the animal, the Book of Jonah concludes with the Lord rejecting Jonah's plea for the destruction of the wicked city of Nineveh with these words: "And should I not care about Nineveh, that great city in which there are more than one hundred and twenty thousand persons... *and many beasts as well*" (*Jonah* 4:11).

Although the prohibition of not eating the limb of a living beast was, according to the Rabbis, one of the seven laws of Noah encumbent upon all mankind, "today," H. Lowe points out, "eels are still skinned alive, cod is crimped and lobsters are boiled unpithed. It is remarkable that Jews did not kill animals for sport. Fish had to be netted. Mr. William Radcliffe in his book, *Fishing From Earliest Times*, blames Jews for lacking the sporting spirit. They caught fish by net; they did not play them with the rod. The word 'hook' occurs in the Bible only as a metaphor of cruelty, or as an instrument used by foreigners."

Upon putting on a piece of clothing for the first time, the Jew is instructed to recite a special benediction: "Blessed art Thou, O Lord our God, Sovereign of the Universe, Who hast kept us in life, and hast preserved us, and hast enabled us to reach this season." An exception is made, however, in the case of shoes, for they are made of leather, and the life of an animal had to be taken to fashion them.

This, in fact, is the reason given in the book, *Haminhagim,* for the prohibition against wearing shoes on Yom Kippur:

> Rabbi Moses Isserles wrote: "It is the custom to say to a person putting on a new garment, 'May you wear it out and get a new one.' There are some who write that one ought not to say this about shoes or clothing which are made from the skin of animals (even if unclean), for it would seem as though the animal were being killed to make a garment...[And] on the day of grace and compassion, Yom Kippur, how can one wear shoes which require taking the life of an animal, for it is written, 'His tender mercies are over all His works'(Ps. 145:9)? "[8]

Shmuel Agnon relates how shortly after the turn of the century he met an old *shoḥet* of about eighty, who came from the town where the famed founder of Hasidism, Yisroel Baal Shem Tov, had served as a *shoḥet* for several years as a young man, for in those days he dwelt in obscurity and was engaged in various menial occupations. "Did you ever hear of anyone who actually saw the Baal Shem," inquired Agnon. "Not a Jew," was the reply, "but a gentile. I will tell you about it. I worked on a large farm next to a farm owned by a gentile. One day I was whetting the stone on which I sharpened my slaughtering knife, when the gentile farmers' ancient grandfather, close to a hundred years of age, who was observing me, began to shake violently. I noticed that this happened several times when I was whetting the stone. I did not know whether he was just shaking from old age or shaking his head in disapproval of something I was doing. The next time this happened, I asked him if I was doing something he did not approve of, and this is what he said:

> 'When Yisroelke* would whet his stone, he did so with his tears!' "9

Milk and meat. The earliest understanding of the verse, "Thou shalt not cook a kid in its mother's milk," already took it in the larger sense of separation of milk and meat. According to Maimonides, the biblical prohibition had its origin in the fact that the pagan cults of Canaan practiced a fertility rite which was particularly abominable and which revolted the Jews: the cooking of a kid in its mother's milk. A further reason for the prohibition, suggested Abraham Heschel, may be that the goat — for us more commonly the cow — generously and steadfastly provides us with the single most perfect food we possess: milk. It is the only food which, by reason of its proper composition of nutrients, can by itself sustain the human body. How callous we would be to take the child of an animal to whom we are so indebted and cook it in the very milk which nourishes us and is given us so freely by its mother.

The Human Animal. A final word about the lesson of

---

*Yisroel Baal Shem Tov

reverence for life which *kashrut* teaches, perhaps the most important word of all. We have remarked that the practice of *kashrut* serves to tame and control our aggressive nature regarding animals. But where does one draw the line? To stalk a deer and hunt it down or to stalk a human and hunt him down may not be greatly different.

Jacob Milgrom has written: "The sight of blood, the rattle of death and the glassy stare contrive to dampen the joy of the first kill, if not to leave the initiate sick to his stomach. To kill for the first time may be an ordeal. Thereafter, however, the protest of the conscience is stifled: after repeated performances, compassion takes flight, love goes into hiding and other emotions fill the vacuum. The prospect of the hunt produces an exultation which henceforth is extended to the prospect of the kill. In the history of man, hunting began as a necessity: in self-defense or for food and clothing. But the means becomes an end: hunting for sport, to kill for the sake of killing, for the sheer pleasure of killing.

"Here is where the teachers of Judaism detected a danger to human society, claiming that he who brings death to a living thing willfully and wantonly is liable, under certain conditions, to bring death to the highest living thing, man. They spoke from personal experience. For they and their fellow Jews lived for centuries as lieges of hunter-sportsmen, and were not infrequently tortured, maimed and murdered with the same skills perfected in the hunt. Furthermore, in the course of their historical experiences, they saw the identical hunting skills applied to the greatest hunt of all, human warfare. And because they saw that war also was governed by gentlemanly rules — whether the Treuga Dei of the middle ages or the rules of the Geneva Conference of the past century — they felt justified in identifying war with the hunt, except that now the entire earth became the hunter's domain and its human occupants his most prized game."[10]

As the sense of reverence for life is dulled, the conscience is blunted, the divine image of humanity is obscured and the hidden beast within emerges. Is this not what we have witnessed in the 20th century and is this not the danger that threatens the world in the 21st century? Destroying human life is one of the most popular themes of the daily "games" which our children play, gun in hand and murder in their eye. Taking human life is the stock in trade of almost every comic book, movie or television program. Over six thousand murders are committed on the television screens throughout the nation on a single day! This is the education our children receive two or three or more of every twenty-four hours. We are living in an age when six million Jews could perish without great concern on the part of the world, because our sense of horror had been deadened; it is an age which has invented a means of burning millions — the crematorium; blowing up millions — the atomic bomb; and a term for annihilating an entire people — genocide. Was there ever a time more in need of the lesson of reverence for life? Nor should it come as any surprise that, with the cheapening of human life, abortion, even in the last trimester, has become an accepted means of birth-control, accounting for one and a half million deaths a year and for the termination of one third of all pregnan-

cies in the United States, or that euthanasia has growing support?

There is hardly a more powerful or more effective
means of teaching the lesson of reverence for life than
the proper observance of the *mitzvah* of *kashrut.* It is a
daily education throughout one's entire lifetime, and is
observed in the privacy of each individual home.
Kashering and *sheḥitah* — not to eat blood and a humane
manner of slaughter — far from being outmoded are among
the most relevant laws of the Jewish tradition. Indeed, if
a new religion were to be created today, such injunctions
might well be among those promulgated for the needs of
the 21st century.

The Purpose of Ritual

To teach reverence for life, not only as a virtue in
behalf of kindness to animals but as a means of preserv-
ing our very civilization, is of no little importance. But
why is a specific ritual necessary? "Ritual," explains Leon
Wieseltier, "is the conversion of essences into acts," and
he contrasts it to the reigning "ideal of epiphany, the thirst
for what Americans call 'peak experiences.'" Peak experiences will peak, to be followed by "an experience of
eschatological disappointment." But ritual is continuous. It is another way of "attacking our temporality," in-
dependent of peak experiences, though, in fact, it may be
the ground for celebration and exaltation.[11]

Albert Schweitzer, the musician-musicologist-theo-
logian, wrote widely about reverence for life, which to him
was the fundamental concept of humanity. Because his
books had a limited influence, he dramatically appealed

to a larger audience by abandoning fame and fortune at the height of his career to take a medical degree and settle in the remotest part of Africa, where he founded and personally directed a hospital for the natives. As he labored beyond the age of eighty and even received the Nobel Peace Prize, Schweitzer knew that despite a growing number of followers, he had succeeded in changing the thinking of only a small number and the lives of even fewer.

Judaism, claiming to possess a surer way, the way of the *mitzvah*, takes the biblical teachings and fixes them into a regular pattern of observance, the habitual repetition of which seeks to produce a better human being. The *mitzvah* of *kashrut* is an eloquent example of this process. The reverence for life which Judaism teaches is not dependent on any one person, be he ever so noble or his writings ever so wise. *Kashrut* is a systematic means of educating the conscience of those who sincerely observe it from early age to death; since ancient times it continues to be practiced in every land where there is a Jewish family and a Jewish home. It is not strange that the Talmud describes the people-Israel as *raḥmanim bnei raḥmanim*, merciful ones and the children of merciful ones. A. Leroy Beaulieu believes that the practice of *kashrut* has contributed to the merciful nature of the Jewish people. "Consider the one circumstance," he wrote almost a century ago, "that no Jewish mother ever killed a chicken with her own hand, and you will understand why homicide is so rare among the Jews." When the Talmud teaches that "one should rather be among the per-

secuted than the persecutors," the supporting reference
it cites from the Bible is one of the laws of *kashrut*: that
only animals which do not prey on other animals, such
as the lamb or the cow, could be brought as sacrifices to
the Temple.

The majority of humankind agrees with the oft-re-
peated verse from the New Testament, "Not that which
goeth into the mouth defileth a man but that which
cometh out of the mouth." Judaism, however, knows that
what goes into the mouth can also defile a person. So it
has created the system of *kashrut*, which has worked an
untold good over the centuries for the people-Israel. The
laws of *kashrut* forbid the eating of blood, limit the kinds
of animals which may be eaten, provide for a humane
method of slaughter and a specially trained slaughterer.
They have helped to achieve Judaism's goal of hallowing
the act of eating by reminding the Jew that the life of the
animal is sacred and may be taken for food only under
prescribed conditions. From this one learns reverence
for life, both animal and human. Eating, then, is not simply a matter of replenishing one's nutrients or even the
occasion for fine dining etiquette — which fork to use or
where to place the napkin — but first and foremost a process of moral education.

Other people engage in diets for their bodies. Israel
has created a diet for the soul. If the first is under-
standable, why not the second?

How We Eat

Earlier, we suggested that Judaism's way of sanctify-
ing the act of eating is more than keeping kosher, more

even than understanding the eating of meat as a compromise to human weakness and need. *Kashrut* is part of
something larger. For it is not only *what* we eat but just
as much *how* we eat. In Judaism they are interrelated.
In a fruitful analogy which Jewish tradition draws upon,
the Talmud likens the table upon which we eat to the
altar of the Temple. So we are bidden to wash our hands
before breaking bread not simply to cleanse them — even
if they are already clean, water must be poured upon
them in the prescribed manner — but because the priests
washed their hands before they offered a sacrifice. And
between the blessing over the washing of the hands and
the blessing over the bread no word is spoken, to allow for
contemplation of what one is about to do. Salt is sprinkled
over the bread with which we begin our meal, because
salt was put upon the ancient sacrifice. Then the prayer,
"Blessed art Thou, O Lord our God, Sovereign of the Universe, Who bringest forth bread from the earth," is recited, reminding us from whence our food comes. After
the meal, Grace is offered in gratitude for our meal, for
the Holy Land, and to bless the members of the house-
hold. While Grace is recited, the knife is covered, because
no knife was allowed to come upon the ancient altar, for
the knife was a sign of war and the altar a sign of peace.
During the meal we are told to speak words of Torah so
that the children and ourselves should be nourished not
only by God's food but by God's word as well. A child is as
much educated by what is heard at the table as by what
is heard in the schoolroom. "Rabbi Simeon said: If three
have eaten at a table and have spoken there no word of

Torah, it is as if they had eaten of sacrifices to dead idols....
But if three have eaten at a table and have spoken there
words of Torah, it is as if they had eaten at the table of
the Lord" (Avot 3:4). One is reminded of Norman Rockwell's
painting of the train station lunchroom where, amidst a
crowded table of eaters, a young boy and his grandmother
bow their heads in prayer, or of the solemn yet joyous
moment at the Thanksgiving Day table which the artist
portrayed more than once.

Today, we have no Temple in Jerusalem, no altar
there, no sacrifices, no priests to minister. But in their
stead is something even greater. For every home can be
a Temple, every table an altar, every meal a sacrifice
and every Jew a priest. And what was formerly an animal
function, a mechanical behavior, is suddenly transformed
into an elaborate ritual full of mystery and meaning.

Judaism ennobles something ordinary and everyday
with a code of *what* to eat and *how* to eat, by teaching us
that every act of life can be hallowed, even the act of eating. As Abraham Heschel wrote, "Perhaps the essential
message of Judaism is that in doing the finite, we can
perceive the infinite." In eating a slice of bread we can
discover God; in drinking a cup of wine we can sanctify
the Sabbath; in preparing a piece of meat we can learn
something of the reverence of life. Our glory as humans
is in our power to hallow, by means of which we not only
overcome the beast within but even surpass the angels.

Concerning Abraham's receiving the three angels and
preparing a meal for them, it is written, "And he stood
above them, under the tree, and they did eat" (Gen. 18:8).

Puzzled by this verse, a disciple of Rabbi Zusya of Hanipol asked if it was not strange that Scripture should say that the man stood *above* the angels.

No, Rabbi Zusya explained. It was not strange at all. The angels are superior to humans, but humans are also superior to the angels. The angels are superior to humans in not being contaminated by the natural world. Humans are superior to the angels precisely because, being part of the natural world, they possess the power to raise up to God the common, natural acts of which angels know nothing. Consider the above verse. The angels have no need of food and, thus, even though they are pure, they are ignorant of the manner in which to hallow the act of eating. But Abraham was a man who knew that even by the way in which we approach our food, we can serve the Almighty. Thus, in this case when he invited them to his table for a meal, Scripture speaks the truth: he did stand *above* them.

One who finds his way to God in the midst of the world is greater than the angels. The angels may be pure because they are free from our world; they come from heaven and are innocent of the tasks, the problems and the vexations that confront humans. They are static; neither rising nor descending in their everlasting splendour. But humans come from earth as well as heaven; possess a body as well as a soul; have evil thoughts as well as good ones; know passion and greed as well as justice and mercy. They are never static but rise and fall and are capable of behaving as the least or the most glorious of creatures. Humans can be purer than the angels because they, and only they, are called upon to raise earth to heaven. Humans are superior to the angels because their task is the greater — to hallow all of life: to conduct business with honesty, to be loving toward spouse and children, to fight for honest government, to treat others as they would be treated, to curb jealousy and improper desire, to act in such a way that even the most common daily deeds become holy deeds. Abraham stood above the angels because he knew something utterly unknown to them, namely, that eating may be hallowed by the thoughts, the intentions, the manners, the blessings and the preparations of the eater.

THE PROBLEM OF DOING

For the modern Jew, following the practice of *kashrut* depends upon two factors: understanding and will-power. We have discussed that *kashrut* is part of Judaism's attempt to hallow the common act of eating; how buying from a kosher butcher who sells meat slaughtered by a *shoḥet*, removing blood from the meat in preparing it for the table, and saying a blessing before and after meals has relevance and meaning, extending holiness to a mechanical function, helping to produce a holy people. Observance is, in a great part, a matter of correct knowledge, of replacing false understanding with a proper one, a matter of the mind.

But, something else is involved in the question of *kashrut*: a matter of the *will*. *Kashrut* has to do with our choice to live as Jews, with a determination that includes commitment and sacrifice, with a state of mind that is clear and firm. It is not only a matter of understanding, central as this is to the issue, but also one of the will to be a Jew.

To Be Holy Means To Be Set Apart

This second consideration, it should be noted, is likewise implied in the meaning of the Hebrew word for holi-

ness, *kadosh*, which the Bible constantly associates with
the dietary laws. It has already been pointed out that the
purpose of *kashrut* is holiness and that holiness means
hallowing, in this case the hallowing of the act of eating.
But *kadosh* has another meaning as well — *to be set apart.*
"I am the Lord your God, Who have set you apart from the
nations. Ye shall therefore separate between the clean
beast and the unclean. And ye shall be holy unto Me; for I
the Lord am holy and have separated you from the other
nations to be Mine" (Lev. 20:24-26). The limitation and
the preparation of certain kinds of meat, the prohibition
of certain kinds of fish or the separation of milk and meat,
all of which is required of the Jewish kitchen and involves a goodly percentage of the laws of *kashrut*, sets Jews
apart from the gentile by providing them with a Jewish
cuisine, a Jewish kitchen and a Jewish table.

While hallowing the act of eating may be acceptable
to most, being set apart from others by virtue of this hallowing is less so. To many the whole idea of a democratic
society in which ghetto walls are broken down and all
peoples and faiths mingle freely militates against such a
formidable food barrier as *kashrut*, which seems to strike
down the ideal of social integration. Seen as a deterrent
to good interfaith relations by the early German Reform-
ers, it was one of the first parts of Jewish Law abandoned
in their attempt to eliminate the non-universalistic aspects of Judaism. Indeed, even those who do keep kosher
homes often do not hesitate to part company with these
observances once they leave the privacy of their homes.
"At home a Jew, in society a man," as the adage of the

Haskalah (the movement of Western enlightenment among the Jews) had it.

Edmond Fleg, the distinguished French author, tells us in his moving autobiography, *Why I Am a Jew,* how, as a young boy, this double standard of a *kashrut* of convenience threatened to drive him from his religion. "Once I was taken on a journey by my parents and at the hotel where we dined the fat and the lean were mixed, and cheese was served after meat. Even ham appeared on the table. My parents ate and permitted me to eat of this forbidden dish. Then the food forbidden at home was no longer forbidden when one was away from home? The law was law no longer?" Such inconsistency on the part of the parent is the surest way to guarantee that the next generation will abandon the dietary laws altogether. Either *kashrut* is taken seriously as a means of singling the people-Israel out as a people set apart for God's service — a regimen having significance not only within the confines of the home but outside the home as well — or it is doomed to extinction.

The alluring power of conformity, which sweeps together into the "accepted" pattern all dissident elements, is nothing new to Jews. The decision to abandon one's distinctiveness and merge into the majority has been an ever-present enticement to this small, foreign and suffering people living for so long on tolerance in another's land. Today, we call it assimilation. The distinction between those who do not give in to these pressures and those who do has been described by sociologists. The contrast between those who act out of their own resources

("inner"-directed) and those who suppress their own feelings and conform to the crowd ("outer"-directed), is ex-
actly what is meant when, discussing the Jews of Alexandria, Spain or Germany, historians spoke of the
assimilationists and the non-assimilationists. The only
difference today is that the trend toward assimilation,
that is, ridding ourselves of distinctive practices, is so
much the greater in America because of the paucity of
anti-Semitism and the easy acculturating factors of de-
mocracy. All this constitutes a powerful force against
the practice of *kashrut,* urging conformity, like-acting, like-
speaking, like-eating, and frowning upon anything in the
way of thought or manner which might cause one to stand
out from the crowd. Thus, understanding the meaning of
kashrut is only half the equation: one must also have the
will to put it into practice.

Kashrut in Jewish History

The people-Israel possessed the will to observe the
laws of *kashrut* in the past. So strong has their will been
to do so that they believed it worthy of great sacrifice,
even, at times, the greatest sacrifice. Consider for a moment the role which *kashrut* has played in Jewish history. At the time of the Maccabees, part of the Greek persecution consisted of attempting to force the desecration
of the dietary laws upon the Jews. The aged scribe Eleazar,
one of the first recorded martyrs, submitted to death rather
than permit pig's flesh to pass his lips. The record of the
observance of these ritual prescriptions and of the self-
sacrifice that was willingly undertaken for their sake is
closely bound up with the whole subsequent course of

Jewish history. Josephus tells us of the Essenes at the time of the great war against the Romans. "Racked and twisted, burnt and broken, and made to pass through every instrument of torture, in order to induce them to blaspheme their lawgiver or to eat some forbidden thing, they refused to yield to either demand, nor even once did they cringe to their persecutors or shed a tear." Philo speaks of similar episodes in Alexandria. And so, too, later generations suffered under different skies and in different circumstances.

The Marranos of Spain, forced to convert publically but remaining secret Jews, risked their lives to procure meat that was kosher. So damming a sign of heresy was it considered by the Inquisition, that it could bring the death-sentence. Nevertheless, certain of them, when arrested by the Holy Office, managed to observe the dietary laws in the very dungeons in which they were immured. Thus a certain Francisco Maldanado da Silva, who was burned alive in Lima in 1639, refused to touch meat all the long years during which he lay in the condemned cell awaiting his fate; and this is not the only case. Earlier, at the time of the Crusades, when many Jews were dragged to the baptismal font, they nevertheless clung to their ancestral practice. "It is fitting that I should recount their praise," writes a contemporary chronicler, "for whatever they ate.... they did at the peril of their lives. They would ritually slaughter animals for food according to the Jewish tradition" (Roth). There are also miraculous tales of Jewish boys who were forcibly taken into the Russian army at a tender age by Czar Nicholas, separated from their families, raised in distant lands as soldiers, beaten and starved to make them abandon their Jewish ways, and who nevertheless refused to eat forbidden food. To this could be added many tales of spiritual heroism during the period of Nazi and Communist persecution of our own time. Apart from all these examples of endangering one's very life is the day-to-day sacrifice which our people have made without question, complaint or any claims to heroics, in the ordinary course of their affairs: when they happened to be away from home on a trip or if they lived in a small village and had to travel many miles to purchase kosher meat or the countless other cases in the ordinary life of the people-Israel when they overcame difficulties in order to fulfill the *mitzvah* of *kashrut.*

The weight of Jewish history weighs heavy upon the people-Israel. The Talmud says that those *mitzvot* for which they had to suffer became especially dear to them. The *mitzvah* of *kashrut* is undoubtedly an example.

Particularism and Universalism

Perhaps Jews have been selling Judaism too cheaply of late, pruning it of seeming unpleasantries, hiding from the American Jew what the real demands of their faith are, candy-coating it, making it sweet to the taste, pleasant to the eyes, something that lends a shade of brightness and color to whatever kind of person you may happen to be. The real challenge of tradition is glossed over; the rigorous demands of Jewish Law go unmentioned, *kashrut* among them.

The truth is, however, that Judaism does make demands, stern, difficult, almost impossible demands. Judaism proposes a strict discipline which has produced, for those who accept the yoke of the law, a special kind of person and a peculiar kind of people. Such results do not come about from pious platitudes. The prophets' claim is not peace of mind, but that the God of Israel spoke to all mankind through Israel, that they are God's messengers, the keepers of that heritage for all posterity. Destroy the people and you destroy that heritage, for it is not embodied in any book or idea but in the people's living reality.

There is no denying that Jews are a narrow, nationalistic people. One only needs to read the first part of the *Alenu* prayer which is recited at the close of every Jewish service (except in the Reform Movement, which found its particularism too offensive):

> It is our duty to praise the Lord of all things...
> That He hath not made us like the nations of other lands,
> And hath not placed us like other families of the earth,
> That He hath not assigned unto us a portion as unto them,
> Nor a lot as unto all the multitude.
> We bend the knee and offer worship and thanks
> Before the supreme King of Kings, the Holy One, blessed be He.

The severe particularism of the people-Israel is nowhere better expressed than in these words. They contain part of good Jewish doctrine, proclaiming the people's separateness, and their thankfulness for that separateness. But is this separateness an end in itself? Survival for the sake of survival, continuity for the sake of conti-

nuity? Is the people-Israel only particularistic? The answer is found in the second paragraph of the same prayer:

> We therefore hope in Thee, 0 Lord our God,
> That we may soon behold the glory of Thy might,
> When Thou wilt sweep away every false god.
> We hope for the day when the world will be per-
> fected
> Under the kingship of the Almighty,
> And all mankind will call upon Thy name;
> When Thou wilt turn unto Thyself all the wicked
> of the earth. Then all who live will know
> That unto Thee every knee must bend,
> Every tongue vow loyalty.
> May they all accept the yoke of Thy kingship,
> And do Thou rule over them speedily and forever-
> more.
> For the kingdom is Thine,
> And to all eternity Thou wilt reign in glory.
> As it is written in Thy Torah:
> The Lord shall be King over all the earth;
> On that day the Lord shall be one and His name
> one.

The loftiest, most universal utterance in Jewish lit-
urgy is thus joined to the most particularistic. And what
is true of this prayer is true of all of Judaism. Particularism and universalism go hand in hand. This is the message of the Bible and the Talmud, the Prophets and the
Rabbis. A small, peculiar people, Israel, strives through
much of its ritual to preserve itself; yet the end is not
simply self-preservation — why be a Jew and suffer on
that account? — but to be a witness to God amidst the
follies and idolatries of mankind, to prepare for the day
when the world would be perfected under the kingdom of

the Almighty, when every knee would bend and every tongue pledge loyalty, when God alone would rule, when God's name would be truly one. Particularism and universalism, both are essentials of Judaism. Destroy one and you destroy both.

There have been times in Jewish history when the universal aspect of Judaism has almost been forgotten, as is the danger among the ultra-Orthodox in America and in the land of Israel today. There have been times when the particularistic aspect of Judaism was almost forgotten, as is the danger in much of the Jewish world today. In either case a ruinous blow will have been leveled at the integrity of Judaism.

> Ye are My witnesses, saith the Lord;
> And My servant whom I have chosen.
> I the Lord have called thee in righteousness,
> And have taken hold of thy hand,
> And kept thee and set thee for a covenant of the
>   people,
> For a light to the nations;
> To open the blind eyes,
> To bring out the prisoners from the dungeon,
> And them that sit in darkness out of the prison-
>   house.
> (Isa. 43:10; 42:6-7)

Holiness means to hallow our lives; it also means to be set apart for the Lord. Thus one of the primary functions of *kashrut* is to distinguish us from others, to separate us from the nations, to preserve us amidst the maelstroms of history. This must be said clearly and unashamedly. And such separation is just as necessary today as ever before. The logic involved is clear: if Juda-

ism has a role to play in the world, then there must be
Jews to bring it about. For Judaism is not an abstract
creed but a living reality. But the Jews are a small people
scattered amongst the nations. How can they be prevented
from being swallowed up in the course of time? *Kashrut*
helps to distinguish and preserve them, to remind them
three times a day who they are and what God expects of
them. A gentile prophet spoke better than he knew when
he said of Israel: "Lo, it is a people that shall dwell alone,
and shall not be reckoned among the nations" (Num. 23:9).

Milgrom points out that the biblical record of the dietary laws concludes with the words: "You shall be holy to
me, for I the Lord am holy and have set you apart (*hivdalti*)
from other peoples to be mine" (Lev. 20. 24-26). Indeed,
the verb "to separate" (*hivdil*) is used three more times in
these two verses to emphasize the point. "Israel's attain-
ment of holiness is dependent on setting itself apart from
the nations. The dietary system is thus a reflection and
reinforcement of Israel's election."[12] Furthermore,
Milgrom continues, this passage follows the powerful de-
nunciation of the Canaanite and Egyptian sexual practices, implying a connection between sex and food, both
expressions of holiness and both instruments of separation from others.

This separation was of particular moment in the later
Greek and Roman times, when the people-Israel came
under the powerful influence of these cultures, and was
a part of the Roman Empire. Pagan sexual practices were
found to be particularly offensive. One contemporary writer
summed up the connection between the biblical sexual

and dietary prohibitions as a bulwark against these intrusions:

> [The dietary laws teach that] we are set apart from all men. For most of the rest of mankind defile themselves by their promiscuous unions, promoting much depravity, whole countries and cities priding themselves on these vices. Not only do they have intercourse with males, but they even defile mothers and daughters. Nevertheless, we kept apart from such things. (Letter of Aristeas 151-2).

By abolishing the dietary laws as one of their first decrees, Christianity meant not only to ease the way for pagans to convert but to abolish the distinction between gentile and Jew, "to end once and for all the notions that God had covenanted himself with a certain people who would keep itself apart from all the other nations."[12]

Kashrut is one of the firmest ramparts of the particularistic aspect of Judaism. It demands sacrifice, self-discipline and determination, but what in life that is truly worthwhile does not? It demands the courage to turn one's face against the powerful current of conformity, not only against the gentile world as in the past (that was difficult enough, yet in doing so, one could always feel part of a united people), but against part of the Jewish world as well, thus standing witness to God amidst our own people as well as the "peoples." Is this not, however, what the prophet Isaiah, who spoke of his people as God's "witness" and "servant," meant when he sang of a "saving remnant" of Israel? Throughout the Jews' long history — from Egypt to Palestine to Babylonia to Spain to Germany to America to the Land of Israel — it has always been that loyal "rem-

nant," and not the entire nation, who have been faithful
to their task and preserved their heritage. The weight of
the centuries which the Jews carry in their soul endows
them with fortitude. The yoke of the *halakhah,* the "way,"
determines their course. The long chain of tradition to
which the people-Israel is bound and to which it yearns
to add one more link, guides its path — while before its
eyes is framed the glorious vision of the end of time when
all nations will be one and peace will reign. If the Jew is
to say "yes" to the grandeur of Jewish tradition, he must
have the courage to say "no" to the allurements of the
world despite their captivating call to conformity. The problem of *kashrut,* then, is very much involved with the will
to live as a Jew.

To summarize, we may say that the goal of *kashrut* is
holiness, a holy person and a holy nation. It is a part of
Judaism's attempt to hallow the common act of eating
which is an aspect of our animal nature. It likewise sets
the Jew apart from the nations. Thus it achieves its ob-
jective, holiness, in these two ways, both of which are
implied in the Hebrew word, *kadosh,* inner hallowing and
outer separateness. Finally, *kashrut* makes two demands
upon the modern Jew: understanding of the mind and
commitment of the will. Both are indispensable.

According to Aristotle's pupil Clearchus, his master
once had discourse with a Jew and came away impressed
with two things about this people: their admirable philosophy and their strict diet.

Philosophy and diet, thought and practice, inner attitude and outward observance, *agadah* (legend) and *halakhah* (Jewish law) — this combination has characterized Judaism since earliest times. It is the very essence of the Jewish religion.

NOTES

[1]Martin Buber, *Hasidism and Modern Man.* New York: Horizon Press, 1958, pp. 28, 29.

[2]See Samuel H. Dresner, *The Sabbath.* New York: The Burning Bush Press, 1970.

[3]Examples of asceticism are not absent from Judaism. Nahman of Bratslav, the noted Hasidic leader, recommended swallowing one's food whole without mastication in order to go without experiencing the pleasure of eating! The weight of normative Judaism, however, firmly opposed such extremes.

[4]*Bereishit Rabba* 33:3, *BT Bava Metzia* 85a.

[5]"The commandment concerning the slaughtering of animals is necessary," writes Maimonides, "because the natural food of man consists of vegetables and of the flesh of animals.... No physician has any doubts about this. Since, therefore, the desire of procuring good food necessitates the slaying of animals, the Law enjoins that the death of the animal should be the easiest. It is forbidden to torment the animal by cutting the throat in a clumsy manner, by poleaxing, or by cutting off a limb whilst the animal is alive. It is also prohibited to kill an animal with

its young on the same day (Lev. 22:28), in such a manner that the young is also in the sight of the mother; for the pain of the animals under such circumstances is very great, their being no difference in this case between the pain of man and the pain of other living beings, since the love and tenderness of the mother for her young ones... exists not only among humans but among most living beings" (*Guide of the Perplexed*, Friedlander and Pines translation, Part III, chapter 48, p. 253 [Friedlander].)

[6]Jacob Milgrom, *Leviticus 1-16, The Anchor Bible*. New York: Doubleday, 1991, pp. 705-707.

[7]Fritz Stern, *Einstein's Germany*, Princeton University Press, 1999, p.194.

[8]S. Agnon, *Days of Awe*. New York: Schocken Books, 1948, pp. 200-201.

[9]S. Agnon, *Eilu V'eilu*. Tel Aviv: Schocken, 1958, p. 361.

[10]Jacob Milgrom, "Jews Are Not Hunters," *The Reconstructionist*, Oct. 2, 1959, pp. 27-30. I have drawn upon this provocative article at length in this section, and in the following one, "The Purpose of Ritual," Cf. Jacob Milgrom, *Leviticus 1-16,* pp. 641-742.

[11]Leon Wieseltier, *Kaddish*. New York: Knopf, 1998, pp. 68, 69.

[12]Milgrom, *Leviticus 1-16*, pp. 724-727.

THE JEWISH DIETARY LAWS

A GUIDE TO OBSERVANCE

Though the system of the Dietary Laws may at first seem complex, once three basic principles are understood — (1) that only permissible animals and fishes may be eaten; (2) that meat and fowl must be slaughtered and prepared in a certain way; and (3) that meat and dairy foods, including the dishes and utensils used for cooking and eating, cannot be mixed — the person who observes *kashrut* soon finds that it becomes second nature to plan meals, acquire kitchen equipment, do the grocery shopping, and manage the kitchen.

BASIC DEFINITIONS

Kosher (kasher, Hebrew) — Fit or proper for use.

Kashrut (Hebrew) — The system of Jewish Dietary Laws.

Treif (Yiddish) or ***Treifah*** (Hebrew) — The opposite of kosher, as applied to food; not suitable for use; forbidden.[1]

Meat (*fleishig*, Yiddish) — Any meat or poultry product or a product containing a meat derivative.

Dairy (*milchig*, Yiddish) — Any milk or milk-based food or a product containing a milk derivative.

Pareve (Yiddish) — Neither meat nor dairy; "neutral"; i.e., all fish, eggs, fruits, vegetables, and grains.

— — — — — — — — — — —

SEPARATION OF MEAT AND DAIRY FOODS

The law against mixing meat and dairy foods origi-
nates in the Bible, "You shall not boil a kid in its mother's
milk."[2] (See p. 25 for a discussion of the meaning of this
law.) The Rabbis of the Talmud interpreted this verse to
mean that no food product from animals should come in
contact with milk or a milk product. From this basic principle the following rules are derived:

Foods

1. Meat and milk products may not be cooked together or eaten together at the same meal.*

2. Artificial dairy products should have a *pareve*,
kosher rabbinic certification if they are to be used
at a meat meal.**

3. Dairy and meat foods should not be cooked in an
enclosed oven at the same time, but meat and dairy
foods may be cooked on the stove in separate pots at
the same time.

4. Dairy products may not be eaten immediately
after eating meat. The length of time one waits after eating meat before eating dairy products is a
matter of custom: Among Jews from Western Eu-

— — — — — — — — — —

* This rule requires that caution be taken with baked goods
and other prepared or processed foods. Bread, cake, cookies,
and other desserts to be eaten at a meat meal should not
contain milk, butter, or milk derivatives such as casein.

** Margarine, creamers, dessert toppings and the like may contain milk or milk derivatives.

rope, three hours; Jews from Eastern Europe, six hours; Jews from Holland, 72 minutes.[3] If "the tradition of our ancestors" is not known, an individual should establish his or her own tradition, keeping in mind the practice of one's own community.

5.   Meat may be eaten after eating dairy foods.* If it is being eaten at the same table, it is desirable to change the tablecloth or placemat.

6.   *Pareve* or "neutral" foods — fish, eggs, fruits, vegetables, and grains —may be eaten at both dairy and meat meals.**

7.   The principle of separation between meat and dairy is observed by keeping separate dishes, pots and utensils. The exact requirements are discussed in the next section.

THE KOSHER KITCHEN

Basic Requirements

The basic requirements for having a kosher kitchen are that there should be nothing non-kosher in it, and that it should provide for separation of meat and dairy foods and utensils.

— — — — — — — — — —

* One should eat a small portion of bread and drink some liquid to clean the mouth.

** The practice of Jews who have Ashkenazi (European) ancestry, is that *pareve* foods cooked by themselves in a pot used for meat may be served at a dairy meal but not on the same plate with milk products. *Pareve* foods cooked by themselves in a pot used for dairy may be served at a meat meal but not on the same plate with meat products.

If it has been a *treif* or non-kosher kitchen, all traces of non-kosher food must be removed; utensils should be cleaned and "kashered." This process does take work and time but it permits you to use most of your once *treif* (not kosher) kitchen utensils and equipment. What cannot be kashered cannot be kept for use in a kosher kitchen.

Making Things Kosher

The process of kashering is used for three different purposes: (1) converting a kitchen from non-kosher to kosher, (2) preparing a kitchen for Passover, and (3) "purifying" a utensil that has accidentally become non-kosher. The two basic methods of kashering are (1) immersion in boiling water, or purging, and (2) exposure to open flame.

What Can Be Kashered

- Ranges and ovens
- Refrigerators and freezers
- Microwave ovens which do not have a browning element
- Sinks
- Dishwashers
- Counters and tabletops
- Most metal cooking utensils: pots, pans, flatware, and other kitchen ware
- Utensils with Teflon or other nonstick surfaces
- Wooden bowls, unless they would be damaged by the heat of the kashering process
- Plastics with high heat tolerance
- Glassware
- Ovenproof ceramics such as Pyrex, Corningware,

and Corelle
● Many small appliances (mixer, can opener, blender, processor, etc). The determinant is whether the parts that come in contact with food, such as the beaters, blades, and containers, can be immersed in boiling water. If they cannot, the appliance cannot be kashered.

What Cannot Be Kashered?

● Microwave ovens which have a browning element
● Melmac or other plastics that would melt if exposed to the required heat
● Earthenware and other unglazed pottery since the material is absorbent and thus cannot be purged
● Most porcelain or other glazed pottery (china and fine porcelain which have not been used for twelve months are considered as new[4])

Kashering Utensils

Purging: Most cooking utensils used on top of the stove can be made kosher by immersion in boiling water. This includes metal pots and pans (excluding frying pans), flatware, plastic with high heat tolerance, and many other kinds of kitchen ware. The procedure is as follows:

1. The article to be kashered is thoroughly scoured and not used for 24 hours. After which it is completely immersed in a pot of boiling water and is then rinsed under cold water.*
2. The pot in which the articles were kashered is then itself kashered.

--- --- --- --- --- --- --- --- --- ---

* If a pot is too large to fit into another pot, the pot to be kashered is filled to the brim with water and the water is brought to a boil and caused to spill over the sides.

Open Flame: Utensils which come in direct contact with fire and upon which food is cooked directly, such as a barbecue spit, a barbecue grill, a broiling pan, baking tins or pans, and racks are kashered by open flame. A pot or pan which is used in the oven is considered to be in direct contact with fire. The procedure is as follows:

> The article to be kashered is thoroughly scoured and not used for 24 hours, and then put under or over an open flame and thoroughly heated until the metal glows red hot.*

Glassware: Glassware (including ovenproof ceramics) when washed may be considered as new.[5]**

Kashering Appliances

Ranges and ovens: The stove-top is scoured. The heating units are then turned on full for 45 minutes. Self-cleaning ovens are kashered by running a full cleaning cycle.***

Microwave ovens: After the microwave oven has been cleaned, a cup of water is placed in the oven. The oven is

— — — — — — — — — —

* Frying pans need only be heated until the point when a piece of paper is singed when it is touched to the metal.

** However, many Ashkenazi Jews (Jews with European ancestry) kasher glassware by soaking it for 72 hours, changing the water every 24 hours, and will not kasher ovenproof ceramics once they have been used.

*** A non-self-cleaning oven is kashered by thoroughly scouring it, leaving it unused for 24 hours and then running it at the highest temperature for 45 minutes.

turned on and the water is "cooked" until it boils, filling the chamber with steam.

Refrigerators/Freezers: The shelves and bins are removed in order to facilitate cleaning. The shelves, bins, and walls are then washed.

Sink: A metal sink is kashered by thoroughly cleaning it, not using it for 24 hours, and pouring boiling water from a pot or kettle over the whole sink, including faucets and top. The same process is used on porcelain sinks to prepare them for use, but it does not kasher them. **Therefore, in porcelain sinks, racks or tubs need to be used for dishwashing.**

Dishwashers: The interior of the dishwasher is cleaned, paying careful attention to the strainer over the drain. The dishwasher is left unused for 24 hours and then run through a wash cycle with soap.

Small Appliances: Any metal surface of a small appliance that comes in contact with food should be kashered by purging. Plastic parts that can tolerate high heat should also be immersed. Many electrical appliances cannot be immersed and therefore cannot be kashered. An electric mixer should have its beaters purged, and its bowls either purged (metal) or washed (glass). An electric can opener should have its blade and magnets removed and purged. The rest of the appliance should be cleaned so that no food is left in any crevices.

Kashering Countertops and Tables

Countertops and tables made of Formica or Arborite should be washed. Those made of wood are scraped, as well, with a steel brush. The surface is then left bare for 24 hours. After that the surface is splashed with boiling water, poured directly from the pot.*

Separating Meat and Dairy Utensils

The principle of separating between meat and dairy applies to all utensils used in the preparation and consumption of food. This is necessary because various materials are deemed to absorb the flavor (characteristic) of a food. If meat is cooked in a pot used for milk, for example, it is considered the same as mixing the two kinds of food, which is forbidden.

In practical terms, this means that a kosher home has to have at least two sets of dishes, flatware, pots, pans and cooking implements. As a general rule, whatever is used for meat may not be used for dairy and vice versa. It is also desirable to store meat and dairy utensils in separate areas.**

Glassware: Glass is not absorbent and is not deemed to retain the taste (characteristic) of food with which it comes in contact. Therefore, technically, one set of glass dishes could be used for meat and dairy interchangeably.[6]

———————————

*For Passover, it is customary to cover all surfaces with paper, plastic, or other material.

**Since different dishes, etc., must be used during Passover, additional utensils are needed for that purpose. However, flatware and certain other items used during the year can be kashered for Passover use. See the section on Passover for details, p. 68.

But, this practice is discouraged on at least two grounds. One, the use of the same dishes for everything could lead to mixing other utensils. Second, while glass might satisfy the letter of the law, the spirit of the law calls for making a clear distinction between the two categories, dairy (*milchig*) and meat (*fleishig*). The same glassware can be used at dairy and meat meals for cold beverages and foods, such as salads and desserts.

Heatproof ceramics, such as Pyrex and Corningware, are considered the same as glass. [7]

Correcting a Mistake: If a pot, dish, or other utensil has accidentally been used for the wrong category and heat is present, it must be kashered.

Dishwashing

● Meat and dairy utensils should not be washed together (a double sink comes in handy for this purpose).

● If the sink is not a double metal one, separate sink racks or tubs should be used for each category.

● Separate dish towels, dish cloths and scouring pads should be used and clearly identified (usually by using different colors) for meat and dairy.

● Soaps and dishwashing detergents should indicate that they have been produced with rabbinic supervision.

Using the Dishwasher

A dishwasher may be used for both dairy and meat dishes under the following conditions:

● Dairy and meat dishes should not be washed together.
● Dishes should be rinsed before being loaded into the
dishwasher.
● The machine should be run through a full cycle with
soap between meat and dairy loads and between dairy
and meat loads.[8]

PERMITTED FOODS

1. All fresh fruits and vegetables are kosher. Due to
the complexity of food manufacturing processes in our
time it is best to use only canned and frozen foods which
have a *hekhsher*, a certification of rabbinic supervision.
If necessary, frozen foods which have no additives may
be used without certification. Sometimes, frozen and
canned fruits or vegetables are prepared with milk products or with non-kosher ingredients such as non-kosher
meat broth. A careful reading of the ingredients is always necessary.

2. All unprocessed grains are kosher. Check the ingredients of processed items such as dry cereals or baked
goods to make sure they have only kosher ingredients
and that they are free of dairy ingredients if they will be
used with a meat meal.

3. All milk and dairy products, including cheese,
which have no non-kosher additives are kosher and do
not require rabbinic supervision.[9]

4. Eggs from kosher fowl are kosher (and *pareve*).

However, because of the prohibition against eating blood, an egg that contains a speck of blood may not be used. Eggs found inside a slaughtered chicken, with or without a shell covering, are considered kosher and *fleishig* (meat), as is the chicken itself.

5.   All fish that have fins and scales are kosher. Excluded, as a group, are all shell fish.

6.   Meat. The Torah defines the types of beasts and cattle considered kosher (Lev. 11:3 and Deut. 14:4). The main distinguishing signs are the cloven hoof and the fact that the animal chews its cud. Accordingly, the meat of cattle (beef and veal), sheep (lamb and mutton), and goats is permitted.[10] The meat of animals such as swine and rabbits is prohibited.

7.   Fowl. Most domestic fowl are kosher, including the following: capon, duck (domestic), goose (domestic), chicken, turkey, guinea fowl, house sparrow, palm dove, partridge, peacock, pheasant, pigeon, Cornish hen, quail, squab, and turtledoves.[11]

MEAT

Buying Kosher Meat

The kosher butcher has a prime role in the observance of *kashrut.* The butcher is the one who purchases meat that is properly slaughtered, removes the forbidden parts of animals, and kashers (soaks and salts) it. The reliability of a kosher butcher should be attested to by your rabbi or, if traveling, the rabbi of a local congrega-

tion. Several brands of kosher meat and poultry products
are now available in supermarkets and other outlets. The
labels of these products should indicate that they have
been supervised by rabbinic authorities.

Shehitah

Permitted animals and fowl (not fish) must be slaughtered according to Jewish ritual requirements by a *shohet,*
whose piety and knowledge of the laws of *kashrut* have
been attested to by rabbinic authorities. (See pp.16-17
and 24-25 for an explanation of Jewish ritual requirements and the *shohet.*)

After the animal has been properly slaughtered, it is
examined for defects which make the animal unfit for
kosher consumption. Meat has to be certified as kosher
by a reliable rabbinic authority. It does not have to be *glatt*
kosher meat.[12]

Preparing Meat for Use (Kashering)

Since it is forbidden to eat the blood of an animal, the
blood must be removed before the meat is cooked. This
process is called kashering and involves either soaking
and salting or broiling. Today, almost all kosher meat
purchased in the United States has been kashered by
the local butcher or kosher meat packaging company. All
frozen meat and poultry produced under rabbinic supervision have already been kashered.

Special Cases

Liver: Because it contains an excessive amount of blood, liver can be kashered *only* by broiling, and should not be soaked. Even if liver is to be cooked some other way, it must first be broiled.

Broiling: Because broiling is considered the most effective procedure for the removal of blood from meat, kosher meat that has not been soaked and salted can be kashered by broiling. The procedure for kashering by broiling is as follows:

1. A small amount of salt (any salt will do) is sprinkled on the meat immediately before broiling.

2. The meat is placed on a grid or rack that lets the blood drip freely during the broiling process. The pan that catches the drippings should be used for no other purpose. The blood drippings are considered *treif.*

3. The meat is broiled long enough so that there is a change of color and a crust is formed.

4.   The meat is then turned, and the other side is salted and broiled.

Broilers

Meat may be broiled in an electric or gas broiler, or over an open fire as on a barbecue. [13] The blood should be allowed to drip freely.

PROCESSED FOODS

Determining Whether a Product is Kosher

Processed foods should have a kosher symbol. The

kosher symbols* will often be accompanied by other designations. The word *"pareve"* is used when no milk or meat products or derivatives are used. The letter "P" (such as KP, O/U P) means that the product is permissible for Passover use. The letter "M" (such as KM) is used when the product is considered dairy (*milchig*) by the rabbinic authority. DE indicates that the product, though *pareve*, was made on dairy equipment and can be served at *fleishig* (meat) meals but not together with meat.

Gelatin and Other Additives

Some substances that originate in animal sources undergo such complete change as a result of chemical treatment that they can no longer be regarded as "meat" products. This is the case with both gelatin and rennet, which Conservative authorities have ruled are kosher. (The Appendix, p. 73, provides an explanation of the legal principles involved.)

Wine

The Committee on Jewish Law and Standards of the Conservative Movement[14] recognizes the defensibility of the view that all wines, brandy, cognac, sherry, vermouth, and champagne are kosher and thus do not require rabbinic certification. However, it recommends only *hekhshered*, rabbinically certified, wines be used because of potential issues in wine production that bear on its

— — — — — — — — —

* The letter "K" is used on many packages and labels to note kosher supervision. Since it cannot be copyrighted, anyone with rabbinical background may use it. Therefore, the *kashrut* of any product using this symbol should be considered unacceptable unless it is investigated further.

kashrut. [15] During Passover, only wine that is certified kosher should be used.

When wine is used for the fulfillment of a *mitzvah,* such as circumcision, weddings, *kiddush* and *havdalah,* it is proper to use wine that is certified kosher. It is further recommended that Israeli wines (all of which are certified kosher) be used.

EATING OUT

Owing to the small number of kosher facilities in many parts of the United States and Canada, the following principles may apply:

1.   Determine whether there are kosher facilities available within a reasonable distance. These facilities might be found in vegetarian or dairy restaurants. Preference should always be given to kosher facilities even when non-kosher facilities are more appealing.

2. If it is necessary to dine in non-kosher facilities, meat and dishes containing meat may not be eaten. Some sanction only the eating of cold foods, such as salads, if the food contains no forbidden ingredients. Others approve eating permitted fish and other foods, even if cooked.

3. S*e'udot shel mitzvah* (e.g., a celebratory meal in fulfillment of a commandment — weddings, *bar mitzvahs,* and *brit* ceremonies) should be kosher.

4. A student choosing a college is advised to inquire about the availability of kosher food or facilities for doing one's own cooking.

5. All national and international airlines will provide kosher or vegetarian meals if requested ahead of time. This is also true of many hospitals, hotels and resorts.

6. Jews wishing to observe the dietary laws in the armed services should see their chaplain.

OTHER TRADITIONS REGARDING EATING

The Jewish home is sanctified by the observance of *kashrut* (see pp. 30-31). In addition to the regulations concerning food, the table itself is regarded as an altar of holiness. In order to realize this goal, Jewish tradition has prescribed the following:

1. *Ritual Washing of the Hands*: Washing the hands is not only a hygienic measure, it is also a religious ceremony. Therefore, a special blessing has been ordained to be recited immediately before drying the hands. The water should be poured on the hands from a glass or some other vessel. The blessing is:

Barukh Atah Adonai, Eloheinu Melekh ha'olam, asher kidd'shanu b'mitzvotav, v'tzivanu al n'tilat yadayim.

Praised are You, Adonai our God, Who rules the universe, instilling in us the holiness of *mitzvot* by commanding us concerning the washing of the hands.

2. *The Blessing Over the Bread*: Immediately after washing the hands (without any interruption,

even of talking), a blessing should be pronounced over the bread.

Barukh Atah Adonai, Eloheinu Melekh ha'olam, hamotzi lehem min ha'aretz.

Praised are You, Adonai our God, Who rules the universe, bringing forth bread from the earth.

If one pronounces this blessing it is not ordinarily necessary to pronounce any other blessing during the meal. It is customary to sprinkle salt on the bread before it is eaten (see pp. 31).

3. *Grace After Meals:* After the meal, Grace is recited. Prior to the recitation of the Grace, it is customary to cover or remove any knives which are on the table (see pp. 31).

COOKING ON *SHABBAT*

Both the tending of fire and cooking are among the biblical prohibitions against work on *Shabbat.* A distinction was made, however, between cooking and warming. The following conditions should be observed:

1. It is permissible only to reheat previously cooked foods.

2. The flame or electric heat should not be raised or lowered on *Shabbat.**

————————————

* If a burner is left on during *Shabbat*, it should be covered with a *blech,* tin plate, to prevent the possibility of inadvertently adjusting the stove or oven.

3. Solids may be warmed at any temperature.

4. Liquids may be warmed as long as the fire is not
    so hot as to raise the liquid to a level that is not
    touchable.

TAKING *HALLAH*

When bread is baked in the home, it is customary to
remove a small portion of the kneaded dough to commemo-
rate the portion given to the priests during the time of
the Temple. The piece taken is usually the size of an
olive, and it is burned in the oven at the same time as
the bread bakes. Dough not burned in the oven is thrown
away. The custom is generally that "*hallah*" should be
taken in any recipe using at least three and a half pounds
of flour. The following blessing is said:

*Barukh Atah Adonai, Eloheinu Melekh ha'olam, asher
kidd'shanu b'mitzvotav, v'tzivanu l'hafhrish hallah.*

Praised are You, Adonai our God, Who rules the
universe, instilling in us the holiness of *mitzvot* by
commanding us to separate *hallah*.

PASSOVER

The Torah prohibits the ownership of _hametz_ (leaven) during _Pesah_. Therefore, we arrange for the sale of the _hametz_ to a non-Jew. The transfer, _mekhirat hametz_, is accomplished by appointing an agent, usually the rabbi, to handle the sale. It is valid and legal transfer of ownership. At the end of the holiday, the agent arranges for the reversion of ownership of the now-permitted _hametz_. If ownership of the _hametz_ was not transferred before the holiday, the use of this _hametz_ is prohibited after the holiday as well (_hametz she-avar alav ha-Pesah_).

Since the Torah prohibits the eating of _hametz_ during _Pesah_, and since many common foods contain some admixture of _hametz_, guidance is necessary when shopping and preparing for _Pesah_.

During the eight days of _Pesah_, _hametz_ cannot lose its identity in an admixture. Therefore, the minutest amount of _hametz_ renders the whole admixture _hametz_ and its use on _Pesah_ is prohibited. However, during the rest of the year, _hametz_ follows the normal rules of admixture, i.e., it loses its identity in an admixture of one part _hametz_ and sixty parts of non-_hametz_ (_batel beshishim_). This affords us the opportunity to differentiate between foods purchased before and during _Pesah_.

What follows is a general guideline. However, your rabbi should be consulted when any doubt arises. Foods with _kosher lePesah_ labels that do not bear the name of a rabbi or one of the recognized symbols of rabbinic supervision, or which are not integral to the package, should not be used without consulting your rabbi.

Prohibited foods include the following: leavened bread, cakes, biscuits, crackers, cereal, coffees containing cereal derivatives, wheat, barley, oats, spelt, rye, and all liquids containing ingredients or flavors made from grain alcohol.

Most Ashkenazic authorities have added the following foods (*kitniyot*) to the above list: rice, corn, millet, legumes (beans and peas; however, string beans are permitted). The Committee on Jewish Law and Standards has ruled unanimously that peanuts and peanut oil are permissible. Some Ashkenazic authorities permit, while others forbid, the use of legumes in a form other than their natural state, for example, corn sweeteners, corn oil, soy oil. Sephardic authorities permit the use of all of the above. Consult your rabbi for guidance in the use of these products.

PERMITTED FOODS

A. The following foods require no *kosher lePesaḥ* label if purchased prior to *Pesaḥ*: unopened packages or containers of natural coffee without cereal additives (however, be aware that coffees produced by General Foods are not kosher for Passover unless marked KP); sugar, pure tea (not herbal tea); salt (not iodized); pepper; natural spices; frozen fruit juices with no additives; frozen (uncooked) vegetables (for legumes see above); milk; butter; cottage cheese; cream cheese; ripened cheeses such as cheddar (hard), muenster (semi-soft) and camembert (soft); frozen (uncooked) fruit (with no additives); baking soda.

B. The following foods require no *kosher lePesaḥ* label if purchased before or during *Pesaḥ*: fresh fruits and vegetables (for legumes see above), eggs, fresh fish and fresh meat.

C. The following foods require a *kosher lePesaḥ* label if purchased before or during *Pesaḥ*: all baked products (*matzah*, cakes, *matzah* flour, *farfel*, *matzah* meal, and any products containing *matzah*); canned or bottled fruit juices (these juices are often clarified with *kitniyot* which are *not* listed among the ingredients — however, if one *knows* there are no such agents, the juice may be purchased prior to *Pesaḥ* without a *kosher lePesaḥ* label); canned tuna (since tuna, even when packed in water, has often been processed in vegetable broth and/or hydrolyzed protein — however, if it is *known* that the tuna is packed exclusively in water, without any additional ingredients or additives, it may be purchased without a *kosher lePesaḥ* label); wine; vinegar; liquor; oils; dried fruits; candy; chocolate flavored milk; ice cream; yogurt; soda.

D. The following processed foods (canned, bottled or frozen), require a *kosher lePesaḥ* label if purchased during *Pesaḥ*: milk, butter, juices, vegetables, fruit, milk products, spices, coffee, tea, and fish, as well as all foods listed in Category C.

DETERGENTS

If permitted during the year, powdered and liquid detergents do not require a *kosher lePesaḥ* label.

MEDICINE

Since *hametz* binders are used in many pills, the following guidelines should be followed: If the medicine is required for life sustaining therapy, it may be used on *Pesah*. If it is not for life sustaining therapy, some authorities permit, while others prohibit. Consult your rabbi. In all cases, capsules are kashered by rinsing.

KASHERING OF UTENSILS

The process of kashering utensils depends on how the utensils are used. According to *halakhah*, leaven can be purged from a utensil by the same process in which it was absorbed in the utensil (see "The Kosher Kitchen," pp. 52-57). Therefore, utensils used in cooking are kashered by boiling, those used in broiling are kashered by fire and heat, and those used only for cold food are kashered by rinsing.

A. **Earthenware** (china, pottery, etc.) may not be kashered. However, fine translucent chinaware which has not been used for over a year may be used if scoured and cleaned in hot water.

B. **Metal** (wholly made of metal) UTENSILS USED IN FIRE (spit, broiler) must first be thoroughly scrubbed and cleansed and then made as hot as possible. Those used for cooking or eating (silverware, pots) must be thoroughly scrubbed and cleaned and completely immersed in boiling water. Pots should not be used for a period of at least 24 hours between the cleaning and the immersion in boiling water. Metal baking utensils cannot be kashered.

C. **Ovens and Ranges**: Every part that comes in contact with food must be thoroughly scrubbed and cleaned. Then, oven and range should be heated as hot as possible for a half hour. If there is a broil setting, use it. Self-cleaning ovens should be scrubbed and cleaned and then put through the self-cleaning cycle. Continuous cleaning ovens must be kashered in the same manner as regular ovens.

Microwave Ovens, which do not cook the food by means of heat, should be cleaned, and then a cup of water should be placed inside. Then the oven should be turned on until the water disappears. A microwave oven that has a browning element cannot be kashered for *Pesah*.

D. **Glassware**: Authorities disagree as to the method for kashering drinking utensils. One opinion requires soaking in water for three days, changing the water every 24 hours. The other opinion requires only a thorough scrubbing before *Pesah*, or putting them through a dishwasher.

Glass Cookware: There is a difference of opinion as to whether it is to be kashered. One opinion is that it must be kashered. After a thorough cleansing, there should be water boiled in them which will overflow the rim. The other opinion is that only a thorough cleansing is required.

Glass Bakeware, like metal bakeware, may not be kashered.

E. **Dishware**: After not using the machine for a period of 24 hours, a full cycle with detergent should be run.

F. **Electrical Appliances**: If the parts that come in contact with *hametz* are removable, they can be kashered in the appropriate way (if metal, follow the rules for metal utensils). If the parts are not removable, the appliances cannot be kashered. (All exposed parts should be thoroughly cleaned.)

G. **Tables, Closets and Counters**: If used with _hametz_, they should be thoroughly cleaned and covered, and then they may be used.

H. **Kitchen Sink**: A metal sink can be kashered by thoroughly cleaning and then pouring boiling water over it. A porcelain sink should be cleaned and a sink rack used. If, however, dishes are to be soaked in a porcelain sink, a dish basin must be used. The racks and dish basins that are used must be used only for _Pesah_.

I. **Hametz and Non-Passover Utensils**: Non-Passover dishes, pots and _hametz_ whose ownership has been transferred, should be separated, locked up or covered, and marked in order to prevent accidental use.

The Rabbinical Assembly Pesah Guide was prepared for the Rabbinical Assembly Committee on Jewish Law and Standards by Rabbi Mayer Rabinowitz. It was accepted by the Committee on December 12, 1984. Parts have been amended to reflect more recent decisions of the Committee affecting the status of peanuts, peanut oil, certain cheeses and canned tuna.

APPENDIX

Additives

Chemical additives to food products present difficult halakhic problems. Many additives are complicated compounds whose origin is difficult to ascertain. They may derive either from milk substances or from animal substances. In the former case, the question is whether they may be used together with meat. In the latter case, the problem involves the source of the animal substance — whether a clean or an unclean animal and whether the derivative can be used with milk products. If you have questions, you should speak to your rabbi.

In approaching these questions it should be noted that, according to the laws of *kashrut*, not everything coming from an animal or a milk source necessarily retains the character of its source. The halakhic principles involved are:

1. *Pirsha b'alamah* — mere secretion. This notion is applied by the Rabbis (*Hulin* 116b) to secretions from the animal which have no food value. The classic example of this is rennet which is used in the curdling of cheese. Though this product may come from the organs of an animal, it ceases being considered an animal substance because it is not a real food but a secretion.

2. *Batel beshishim.* The Rabbis developed the concept
    of *bitul,* annulment. This refers to the fact that
    even if the substance is in itself nonkosher, it is
    present in such minute amounts that it is assimi-
    lated totally into the permitted element and is con-
    sidered as if it did not exist. The amount usually
    required is a ratio of one (forbidden) to sixty (per-
    mitted).

3. *Davar ḥadash.* Sometimes the substance is so
    altered in the process of production that it bears
    little resemblance to the original. In this case, it
    does not share the characteristics of its original
    form. An example of this is gelatin which, though
    coming from an animal substance, is so altered
    in the course of production that it cannot be con-
    sidered in the same category as animal sub-
    stances. [22]

NOTES

A Guide to Observance

[1]The word literally means "torn by a wild beast." See, for example, Exodus 22:30.

[2]Exodus 23:19, 34:26, and Deuteronomy 14:21.

[3]The reasons for the waiting period is that the taste of meat in the mouth lingers and particles of meat sometimes get lodged between the teeth. Because of this, eating a milk product without a sufficient waiting period between eating meat and milk is considered to be the same as eating meat and milk together.

[4]*She'elot U'Teshuvot Hakham Zevi*, #75 and *Medini, Sedeh Hemed*, under *Hametz U'Matzah*, Vol. 7, p. 178.

[5]In regard to glassware, the *Shulhan Arukh* (*Orah Hayim* 451:26) states: "Glass utensils do not require any *'hekhsher'* because they do not absorb." There are differing views, however. Rabbi Moses Isserles (*ad loc.*): "Even purging (glass) is ineffective." Rabbi Abraham Danzig (*Hayei Adam* 124:22) writes that the proper method to kasher glassware is to soak it in clear water for 72 hours, changing the water every 24 hours.

[6]*Orah Hayim* 451:26.

[7]See Rabbi Kassel Abelson's *Responsum on Glass Cookware*. Committee on Jewish Law and Standards.

[8]Klein, *Guide*, pp. 369-370 and Efrati, *Sha'arai Halakhah*, sec. 4, pp. 29-33. Shaul Ovadya in *Magen B'edi* maintains that meat and dairy dishes can be washed in the same machine without the rinse cycle (#19, pp. 102-111).

[9]The status of cheese has been the subject of controversy. Some people eat only cheese that has been rabbinically certified. The point at issue: Is rennet, a substance derived from an animal and used in cheesemaking, actually a meat product or even a food? Some Conservative authorities, and others, have concluded that rennet is not a food product, and thus no rabbinic supervision is needed. For additional information, see Appendix, pp. 73-74, "Additives." The question of cheese is explored by Rabbi Isaac Klein in his book, *Responsa and Halakhic Studies*, pp. 43-58.

[10]The deer is also a permitted animal; however, it would have to be ritually slaughtered in order for the meat to be kosher.

[11]The Bible does not list general principles for distinguishing kosher from non-kosher fowl, but lists forbidden species. The Rabbis of the Talmud derived specific characteristics which all permitted birds have in common.

[12]The term *glatt* means "smooth." It refers to the practice

of using only those animals whose lungs are smooth, free of any *sirkhot* (adhesions). Since the codes of Jewish law indicate which lesions render the animal unfit, and how to determine this, the insistence that all meat be "glatt" seems to be an unnecessary burden on those who observe *kashrut*. Today, it is a code word since there are "glatt kosher" dairy restaurants.

[13]Report of the Committee on Jewish Law and Standards of the Rabbinical Assembly of America, 1953 *Proceedings*, p. 40.

[14] On this subject see Rabbi Israel Silverman in *Conservative Judaism and Jewish Law* (Seymour Siegel, ed.), pp. 308-316.

[15] See Rabbi Elliot N. Dorff's *Responsum on the Use of All Wines*, October, 1985. The Committee on Jewish Law and Standards.

Milton Keynes UK
Ingram Content Group UK Ltd.
UKHW020453261124
3115UKWH00051B/368

9 780838 121054